DEDICATION

Thank you to all of the willing tasters
that have supported me along the way!

Table of Contents — Page

10 Tips for using your air fryer — vi

Air fryer Temperature conversion chart — ix

Recipes

Breakfast

Hard Boiled Eggs — 1
French Toast Fingers — 4
Cinnamon Puff Pastry Rolls — 7
Avocado Eggs — 10

Snacks

Zucchini Fries — 13
Sweet Potato Wedges — 16
Plantain Chips — 19
Onion Rings — 22

Main Dishes And Sides

Herbed Salmon and Green Beans — 25
Lemon Pepper Chicken Wings — 28
Crispy 5-Spice Pork Belly Bites — 31

Spinach And Feta Filo Parcels ... 34

Cajun Shrimp ... 37

Simple Chicken Nuggets ... 40

Chicken Quesadillas ... 43

Corn Cob Ribs ... 46

Roasted Cauliflower ... 49

Desserts

Caramelized Bananas ... 52

Speedy S'mores ... 55

Cinnamon Apple Chips ... 58

My notes ... 61

10 Top Tips for using your air fryer

Are you just starting out on your air fryer journey? Follow these top tips to make the most of your new appliance!

1. **Read the Manual:**

    - Before diving into your air frying adventure, take the time to read the user manual that comes with your specific air fryer model. It provides essential information on operation, safety, and maintenance.

2. **Preheat the Air Fryer:**

    - Just like with an oven, preheating your air fryer before cooking is crucial for achieving optimal results. Preheat for a few minutes at the recommended temperature.

3. **Use the Right Amount of Oil:**

    - While air fryers use less oil than traditional frying methods, it's still important to lightly coat your ingredients with oil if you want them to come out crispy. Use a spray bottle or brush to evenly distribute the oil. A small amount of oil will also help herbs and spices stick to food.

4. **Don't Overcrowd the Basket:**

    - To ensure even cooking and proper air circulation, avoid overcrowding the air fryer

- basket. Cook in batches if necessary, especially for foods like fries and nuggets.

5. **Shake or Flip During Cooking:**
   - To achieve uniform crispiness, shake the basket or flip the food halfway through the cooking time. This helps to ensure that all sides are exposed to the hot air.

6. **Check for Doneness:**
   - Use a meat thermometer to check the internal temperature of proteins to ensure they are thoroughly cooked. For other items, such as fries, check for the desired level of crispiness.

7. **Prevent Sticking:**
   - To prevent food from sticking to the air fryer basket, lightly coat it with oil or use a silicone liner. Make sure to leave space between items to allow hot air to circulate.

8. **Mind the Size of Ingredients:**
   - Cut ingredients into similar sizes to ensure they cook evenly. Smaller pieces may cook faster, while larger pieces may require more time.

9. **Clean Regularly:**

    Regular cleaning is essential for maintaining your air fryer's performance. Most air fryers have dishwasher-safe parts, but always check the manual for specific cleaning instructions. Wipe down the interior and exterior after each use to prevent build-up.

10. **Adjust Cooking Times and Temperatures:**

    - Air fryers can vary in their cooking efficiency, so be attentive to how your specific model performs. If you find that your food is getting too crispy or not crispy enough, adjust the cooking times and temperatures accordingly. Keep a watchful eye, especially during the first few uses, to fine-tune your cooking settings and achieve the desired results.

Remember, using an air fryer is a learning experience, and you'll likely discover new tricks and techniques as you become more familiar with it. Enjoy the process of experimenting and creating delicious, quick and easy meals with your air fryer!

Air fryer temperature conversion chart

One of the greatest things about an air fryer is that it can cook far more quickly than a conventional oven, thanks to its small size and the way it circulates hot air around the food. However, this also means you will have to adjust your cooking times accordingly. Keep this chart handy as an approximate guide to convert oven cooking times to air fryer cooking times.

Oven cooking time	Air Fryer cooking time
10 minutes	8 minutes
15 minutes	12 minutes
20 minutes	16 minutes
25 minutes	20 minutes
30 minutes	24 minutes
35 minutes	28 minutes
40 minutes	32 minutes
45 minutes	36 minutes
50 minutes	40 minutes
55 minutes	44 minutes
60 minutes	48 minutes

Hard-Boiled Eggs

Ingredients:

- Eggs (as many as desired)
- Ice water (in a bowl, for cooling)

Instructions:

1. **Preheat the Air Fryer:**
    - Preheat your air fryer to 250°F (120°C) for about 2-3 minutes.

2. **Prepare the Eggs:**
    - Place the desired number of eggs in a single layer in the air fryer basket. You can cook as many eggs as your air fryer can accommodate, as long as they are in a single layer.

3. **Air Fry:**
    - Place the eggs in the preheated air fryer and cook at 250°F (120°C) for 15 minutes.

4. **Prepare an Ice Bath:**
    - While the eggs are cooking, prepare a bowl of ice water. You'll use this to cool the eggs quickly once they are done cooking.

5. **Cool the Eggs:**
    - Once the cooking time is complete, transfer the eggs immediately to the ice water bath using tongs or a slotted spoon. Let them sit in the ice water for at least 5 minutes to cool completely.

6. **Peel the Eggs:**
   - Gently tap each egg on a hard surface to crack the shell, then roll it to loosen the shell. Peel the eggs under cool running water to make it easier.

7. **Serve or Store:**
   - Once peeled, you can slice the hard-boiled eggs for salads, sandwiches, or enjoy them as a snack. If not using immediately, store the peeled eggs in the refrigerator.

Tips:
- It's a good idea to use eggs that are not extremely fresh for easier peeling.

French Toast Fingers

Ingredients:

- 4 slices of thick-cut bread (such as brioche or challah) cut into 1-inch strips
- 2 large eggs
- 1/2 cup milk
- 1 tablespoon granulated sugar
- 1/2 teaspoon vanilla extract
- 1/4 teaspoon ground cinnamon (optional)
- Butter or cooking spray, for coating
- Maple syrup, powdered sugar, or your favourite toppings

Instructions:

1. **Preheat the Air Fryer:**
    - Preheat your air fryer to 360°F (180°C) for a few minutes.

2. **Prepare the Batter:**
    - In a shallow bowl, whisk together the eggs, milk, sugar, vanilla extract, and ground cinnamon (if using). Mix well until all ingredients are combined.

3. **Soak the Bread:**
    - Dip each piece of bread into the egg mixture, ensuring both sides are well-coated. Allow the bread to soak for about 15-20 seconds, letting it absorb the flavors.

4. **Coat with Butter or Cooking Spray:**
   - Lightly coat the air fryer basket or tray with butter or cooking spray to prevent sticking.

5. **Arrange in the Air Fryer:**
   - Place the soaked bread 'fingers' in a single layer in the air fryer basket or on the tray, ensuring they are not overlapping.

6. **Air Fry:**
   - Cook the French toast in the air fryer at 360°F (180°C) for 8-10 minutes, flipping them halfway through the cooking time. Cook until the French toast fingers are golden brown and crispy on the outside.

7. **Serve Warm:**
   - Once done, transfer the air-fried French toast to a plate. Top with your favorite toppings such as maple syrup, powdered sugar, fresh berries, or a sprinkle of cinnamon.

Cinnamon Puff Pastry Rolls with Cream Cheese Glaze

Ingredients:

For the Cinnamon Puff Pastry Rolls:
- 1 sheet of puff pastry, thawed
- 2 tablespoons unsalted butter, melted
- 1/3 cup brown sugar
- 1 teaspoon ground cinnamon
- 1/2 teaspoon vanilla extract

For the Cream Cheese Glaze:
- 4 ounces (113g) cream cheese, softened
- 1/2 cup powdered sugar
- 2 tablespoons milk
- 1/2 teaspoon vanilla extract

Instructions:

1. **Preheat the Air Fryer:**
    - Preheat your air fryer to 375°F (190°C).

2. **Prepare the Cinnamon Filling:**
    - In a small bowl, mix together the melted butter, brown sugar, cinnamon, and vanilla extract to create the cinnamon filling.

3. **Roll Out the Puff Pastry:**
    - On a lightly floured surface, roll out the puff pastry sheet into a rectangle approximately 12x8 inches or buy it pre-rolled.

4. **Spread the Cinnamon Filling:**
   - Evenly spread the cinnamon filling over the entire surface of the puff pastry.

5. **Roll the Puff Pastry:**
   - Starting from one of the longer edges, tightly roll the puff pastry sheet into a log.

6. **Slice into Rolls:**
   - Using a sharp knife, cut the rolled puff pastry into 1-inch thick slices, creating individual rolls.

7. **Place in the Air Fryer:**
   - Arrange the cinnamon puff pastry rolls in the air fryer basket, leaving space between each roll.

8. **Air Fry:**
   - Air fry the cinnamon rolls at 375°F (190°C) for 8-10 minutes or until they are golden brown and puffed up.

9. **Prepare the Cream Cheese Glaze:**
   - In a mixing bowl, whisk together the softened cream cheese, powdered sugar, milk, and vanilla extract until smooth and creamy.

10. **Drizzle with Cream Cheese Glaze:**
    - Once the cinnamon rolls are done, remove them from the air fryer and let them cool for a few minutes. Drizzle the cream cheese glaze over the warm rolls.

Avocado Eggs

Ingredients:

- 2 ripe avocados
- 4 large eggs
- Salt and pepper, to taste
- Optional toppings: chopped fresh herbs, shredded cheese, hot sauce

Instructions:

1. **Preheat the Air Fryer:**
    - Preheat your air fryer to 350°F (175°C).

2. **Prepare the Avocados:**
    - Cut the avocados in half and remove the pits. If needed, scoop out a small portion of the avocado flesh to create a larger well for the eggs.

3. **Place Avocados in the Air Fryer:**
    - Arrange the avocado halves in the air fryer basket, ensuring they are stable and won't tip over.

4. **Crack Eggs into Avocado Halves:**
    - Carefully crack one egg into each avocado half. If the avocados are small, you may need to remove a bit of the egg white or use medium-sized eggs.

5. **Season with Salt and Pepper:**
    - Sprinkle salt and pepper over each avocado and egg to taste.

6. **Air Fry:**

    - Air fry the avocado eggs at 350°F (175°C) for 12-15 minutes, or until the egg whites are set, and the yolks are cooked to your liking. The cooking time may vary based on your specific air fryer, so monitor the eggs to achieve the desired doneness.

7. **Optional Toppings:**

    - If desired, add optional toppings such as chopped fresh herbs, shredded cheese, or a dash of hot sauce.

Zucchini Fries

Ingredients:

- 2 medium zucchinis, washed and cut into matchsticks or wedges
- 1 cup panko breadcrumbs
- 1/2 cup grated Parmesan cheese
- 1 teaspoon garlic powder
- 1 teaspoon dried oregano
- 1/2 teaspoon onion powder
- 1/2 teaspoon paprika
- 2 large eggs, beaten
- Cooking spray or olive oil for misting

Instructions:

1. **Preheat the Air Fryer:**
    - Preheat your air fryer to 400°F (200°C) for a few minutes.

2. **Prepare the Breading Station:**
    - In a shallow dish, combine panko breadcrumbs, grated Parmesan cheese, garlic powder, dried oregano, onion powder, paprika, salt, and black pepper. Mix well.

3. **Dip Zucchini in Eggs:**
    - Dip each zucchini stick into the beaten eggs, ensuring it is coated on all sides.

4. **Coat with Breadcrumb Mixture:**
    - Roll the egg-coated zucchini in the breadcrumb mixture, pressing the breadcrumbs onto the zucchini to adhere.

5. **Arrange in the Air Fryer Basket:**
    - Place the breaded zucchini fries in a single layer in the air fryer basket, ensuring they are not overcrowded.

6. **Air Fry:**
    - Air fry the zucchini fries at 400°F (200°C) for 10-12 minutes, flipping them halfway through the cooking time. Cook until the fries are golden brown and crispy.

7. **Mist with Cooking Spray:**
    - About halfway through the cooking time, open the air fryer and mist the zucchini fries with cooking spray or lightly drizzle them with olive oil. This helps to enhance the crispiness.

8. **Serve Warm:**
    - Once done, transfer the zucchini fries to a serving plate. Serve them warm with your favorite dipping sauce.

Sweet Potato Wedges

Ingredients:

- 2 large sweet potatoes, washed and scrubbed
- 2 tablespoons olive oil
- 1 teaspoon paprika
- 1/2 teaspoon garlic powder
- 1/2 teaspoon onion powder
- 1/2 teaspoon cumin
- 1/2 teaspoon dried thyme
- Salt and black pepper, to taste
- Optional: 1 tablespoon cornstarch (for extra crispiness)

Instructions:

1. **Preheat the Air Fryer:**
   - Preheat your air fryer to 400°F (200°C) for a few minutes.

2. **Prepare the Sweet Potatoes:**
   - Cut the sweet potatoes into wedges. You can leave the skin on or peel them if you prefer.

3. **Seasoning Mixture:**
   - In a large bowl, combine olive oil, paprika, garlic powder, onion powder, cumin, dried thyme, salt, and black pepper. Mix well. If you prefer extra crispiness, you can also toss the sweet potato wedges with cornstarch at this stage.

4. **Coat the Sweet Potatoes:**
   - Add the sweet potato wedges to the bowl with the seasoning mixture. Toss until the wedges are evenly coated.

5. **Arrange in the Air Fryer Basket:**
   - Place the seasoned sweet potato wedges in the air fryer basket in a single layer, ensuring they are not overcrowded.

6. **Air Fry:**
   - Air fry the sweet potato wedges at 400°F (200°C) for 15-20 minutes, shaking the basket halfway through the cooking time to ensure even cooking. Cook until the wedges are golden brown and crispy.

Feel free to pair these sweet potato wedges with your favorite dipping sauce, such as garlic aioli, sriracha mayo, or a tangy yogurt sauce.

Plantain Chips

Ingredients:

- 2 green plantains, peeled
- 2 tablespoons olive oil
- 1 teaspoon chili powder (optional, for a spicy kick)
- 1/2 teaspoon garlic powder
- 1/2 teaspoon onion powder
- Salt, to taste

Instructions:

1. **Preheat the Air Fryer:**
    - Preheat your air fryer to 375°F (190°C) for a few minutes.

2. **Prepare the Plantains:**
    - Slice the peeled plantains into thin, uniform rounds. You can use a knife or a mandolin for consistent thickness.

3. **Seasoning Mixture:**
    - In a large bowl, combine olive oil, chili powder (if using), garlic powder, onion powder, and salt. Mix well to create a seasoning mixture.

4. **Coat the Plantain Slices:**
    - Add the plantain slices to the bowl with the seasoning mixture. Toss until the slices are evenly coated.

5. **Arrange in the Air Fryer Basket:**
    - Place the seasoned plantain slices in the air fryer basket in a single layer, ensuring they are not overcrowded for optimal crispiness.

6. **Air Fry:**
    - Air fry the plantain slices at 375°F (190°C) for 8-10 minutes, flipping or shaking the basket halfway through the cooking time. Cook until the plantain chips are golden brown and crispy.

7. **Cool and Serve:**
    - Once done, transfer the plantain chips to a plate and let them cool for a few minutes. They will continue to crisp up as they cool.

Breadcrumb-Coated Onion Rings

Ingredients:

- 2 large yellow onions, cut into 1/2-inch rings
- 1 cup breadcrumbs (preferably Panko for extra crunch)
- 1/2 cup all-purpose flour
- 1/2 teaspoon paprika
- 1/2 teaspoon salt
- 1/4 teaspoon black pepper
- 2 large eggs, beaten
- Cooking spray or mist

Instructions:

1. **Prepare the Onions:**

    - Cut the onions into 1/2-inch rings and separate them.

2. **Preheat the Air Fryer:**

    - Preheat your air fryer to 375°F (190°C) for a few minutes.

3. **Prepare the Coating Stations:**

    - In one bowl, mix together the breadcrumbs, paprika, salt, and black pepper. In another bowl, place the all-purpose flour. Have a third bowl ready with the beaten eggs.

4. **Coat the Onion Rings:**
    - Dredge each onion ring in the flour, shaking off excess. Dip it into the beaten eggs, allowing any excess to drip off. Finally, coat the onion ring in the breadcrumb mixture, pressing the breadcrumbs onto the surface to adhere.

5. **Arrange in the Air Fryer Basket:**
    - Place the coated onion rings in the air fryer basket in a single layer, ensuring they do not overlap. You may need to cook in batches depending on the size of your air fryer.

6. **Air Fry:**
    - Air fry the breadcrumb-coated onion rings at 375°F (190°C) for 10-12 minutes, flipping them halfway through the cooking time. Cook until the rings are golden brown and crispy.

7. **Mist with Cooking Spray:**
    - About halfway through the cooking time, open the air fryer and mist the onion rings with cooking spray. This step helps enhance the crispiness.

8. **Serve Warm:**
    - Serve the onion rings warm on their own or with your favorite dipping sauce.

Herbed Salmon and Green Beans

Ingredients:

- 2 salmon fillets
- 1 pound fresh green beans, ends trimmed
- 3 tablespoons olive oil
- 2 cloves garlic, minced
- 1 teaspoon dried thyme
- 1 teaspoon dried rosemary
- 1 teaspoon dried parsley
- Salt and black pepper, to taste
- Lemon wedges, for serving

Instructions:

1. **Preheat the Air Fryer:**
   - Preheat your air fryer to 375°F (190°C) for a few minutes.

2. **Prepare the Herbed Oil:**
   - In a small bowl, combine olive oil, minced garlic, dried thyme, dried rosemary, dried parsley, salt, and black pepper. Mix well to create a herbed oil.

3. **Coat Salmon and Green Beans:**
   - Brush the herbed oil over the salmon fillets, coating them on all sides. Toss the trimmed green beans in the remaining herbed oil until they are well-coated.

4. **Arrange in the Air Fryer Basket:**
    - Place the herbed salmon fillets and coated green beans in the air fryer basket, arranging them in a single layer.

5. **Air Fry:**
    - Air fry the salmon and green beans at 375°F (190°C) for 12-15 minutes, or until the salmon is cooked through and flakes easily with a fork. You can shake the basket or flip the salmon halfway through the cooking time for even cooking.

6. **Serve:**
    - Once done, transfer the herbed salmon and green beans to a serving plate.

7. **Garnish and Enjoy:**
    - Garnish with additional herbs if desired and serve with lemon wedges on the side. Squeeze fresh lemon juice over the salmon and green beans before enjoying.

Lemon Pepper Chicken Wings

Ingredients:
- 2 pounds chicken wings, split at joints, tips discarded
- 2 tablespoons olive oil
- Zest of 1 lemon
- 2 tablespoons lemon juice
- 1 teaspoon black pepper
- 1 teaspoon garlic powder
- 1 teaspoon onion powder
- 1/2 teaspoon salt
- 1/2 teaspoon paprika (optional, for color)
- Lemon wedges, for serving

Instructions:
1. **Preheat the Air Fryer:**
    - Preheat your air fryer to 400°F (200°C) for a few minutes.
2. **Prepare the Lemon Pepper Marinade:**
    - In a large bowl, whisk together olive oil, lemon zest, lemon juice, black pepper, garlic powder, onion powder, salt, and paprika (if using). Mix well to create the marinade.
3. **Coat the Chicken Wings:**
    - Add the chicken wings to the bowl with the marinade. Toss until the wings are evenly coated.

4. **Arrange in the Air Fryer Basket:**
   - Place the marinated chicken wings in the air fryer basket in a single layer, ensuring they are not overcrowded.

5. **Air Fry:**
   - Air fry the chicken wings at 400°F (200°C) for 25-30 minutes, flipping them halfway through the cooking time. Cook until the wings are golden brown and crispy.

6. **Serve:**
   - Once done, transfer the lemon pepper chicken wings to a serving plate.

7. **Garnish and Enjoy:**
   - Garnish with additional lemon zest or black pepper if desired. Serve the wings with lemon wedges on the side for an extra burst of citrus flavor.

Crispy 5-Spice Pork Belly Bites

Ingredients:

- 1 pound pork belly, skin-on, cut into strips or bite-sized pieces
- 1 tablespoon soy sauce
- 1 tablespoon oyster sauce
- 1 tablespoon rice vinegar
- 1 teaspoon Chinese five-spice powder
- 1 teaspoon garlic powder
- 1/2 teaspoon ground white pepper
- 1/2 teaspoon salt
- 1 tablespoon cornstarch
- Cooking spray or oil for misting

Instructions:

1. **Prepare the Pork Belly:**
    - Pat the pork belly pieces dry with paper towels. If the skin is not scored, use a sharp knife to make shallow cuts (score) across the skin side, ensuring not to cut into the meat.

2. **Marinate the Pork:**
    - In a bowl, combine soy sauce, oyster sauce, rice vinegar, Chinese five-spice powder, garlic powder, white pepper, salt, and cornstarch. Mix well to create a marinade. Coat the pork belly

pieces with the marinade, ensuring even coverage. Let it marinate for at least 30 minutes to allow the flavors to penetrate the meat.

3. **Preheat the Air Fryer:**

    - Preheat your air fryer to 400°F (200°C) for a few minutes.

4. **Place in the Air Fryer:**

    - Arrange the marinated pork belly pieces in the air fryer basket in a single layer, leaving space between each piece.

5. **Air Fry:**

    - Air fry the pork belly at 400°F (200°C) for 20-25 minutes, turning the pieces halfway through the cooking time. Cook until the pork belly is crispy and golden brown.

6. **Mist with Cooking Spray or Oil:**

    - About halfway through the cooking time, open the air fryer and mist the pork belly with cooking spray or lightly drizzle them with oil. This helps enhance the crispiness.

Spinach and Feta Filo Parcels

Ingredients:

- 1 cup frozen chopped spinach, thawed and drained
- 1 cup crumbled feta cheese
- 1/4 cup grated Parmesan cheese
- 2 cloves garlic, minced
- 1/2 teaspoon dried oregano
- 1/2 teaspoon dried dill
- Salt and black pepper, to taste
- 10 sheets filo pastry (phyllo dough)
- Cooking spray or melted butter for brushing
- Tzatziki sauce, for dipping (optional)

Instructions:

1. **Preheat the Air Fryer:**
    - Preheat your air fryer to 375°F (190°C) for a few minutes.

2. **Prepare the Filling:**
    - In a bowl, combine the thawed and drained chopped spinach, crumbled feta cheese, Parmesan cheese, minced garlic, dried oregano, dried dill, salt, and black pepper. Mix well to create the filling.

3. **Assemble the Filo Triangles:**
   - Lay out one sheet of filo pastry and lightly brush it with melted butter or cooking spray. Place another sheet on top and repeat until you have a stack of 3 sheets.

4. **Add Filling and Fold:**
   - Place a portion of the spinach and feta filling along one edge of the filo pastry stack. Fold the pastry over the filling, forming a triangle. Continue folding in a triangular shape until you reach the end of the pastry.

5. **Seal the Edges:**
   - Use a little water to seal the edges of the filo triangle to prevent them from opening during cooking. Repeat the process with the remaining filo sheets and filling.

6. **Place in the Air Fryer:**
   - Arrange the assembled filo triangles in the air fryer basket, leaving a little space between each one.

7. **Air Fry:**
   - Air fry the spinach and feta filo triangles at 375°F (190°C) for 10-12 minutes, or until they are golden brown and crispy.

8. **Serve:**
   - Once done, carefully remove the filo triangles from the air fryer and let them cool for a minute.

Cajun Shrimp

Ingredients:

- 1 pound large shrimp, peeled and deveined
- 2 tablespoons olive oil
- 1 tablespoon Cajun seasoning
- 1/4 teaspoon cayenne pepper (adjust to taste)
- Salt and black pepper, to taste
- Fresh parsley, chopped (for garnish)
- Lemon wedges (for serving)

Instructions:

1. **Preheat the Air Fryer:**
   - Preheat your air fryer to 400°F (200°C) for a few minutes.

2. **Prepare the Cajun Seasoning:**
   - In a small bowl, mix together Cajun seasoning, cayenne pepper (if using), salt, and black pepper.

3. **Coat the Shrimp:**
   - In a large bowl, toss the peeled and deveined shrimp with olive oil until they are well-coated. Sprinkle the Cajun seasoning mixture over the shrimp and toss until evenly seasoned.

4. **Arrange in the Air Fryer Basket:**

    - Place the seasoned shrimp in the air fryer basket in a single layer, ensuring they are not overcrowded.

5. **Air Fry:**

    - Air fry the Cajun shrimp at 400°F (200°C) for 8-10 minutes, shaking the basket halfway through the cooking time. Cook until the shrimp are pink, opaque, and have a nice sear.

6. **Garnish and Serve:**

    - Once done, transfer the Cajun shrimp to a serving plate. Sprinkle with fresh chopped parsley and serve with lemon wedges on the side.

Simple Chicken Nuggets

Ingredients:

- 1 pound boneless, skinless chicken breasts, cut into bite-sized pieces
- 1 cup breadcrumbs (Panko or seasoned breadcrumbs)
- 1/2 cup grated Parmesan cheese
- 1 teaspoon garlic powder
- 1 teaspoon onion powder
- Salt and black pepper, to taste
- 2 large eggs, beaten
- Cooking spray or mist

Instructions:

1. **Preheat the Air Fryer:**

    - Preheat your air fryer to 375°F (190°C) for a few minutes.

2. **Prepare the Coating Stations:**

    - In a shallow bowl, combine breadcrumbs, grated Parmesan cheese, garlic powder, onion powder, salt, and black pepper. Mix well to create the coating mixture. In another bowl, place the beaten eggs.

3. **Coat the Chicken Nuggets:**
   - Dip each piece of chicken into the beaten eggs, allowing any excess to drip off. Coat the chicken with the breadcrumb mixture, pressing the coating onto the surface to adhere.

4. **Arrange in the Air Fryer Basket:**
   - Place the coated chicken nuggets in the air fryer basket in a single layer, ensuring they do not touch or overlap. You may need to cook in batches depending on the size of your air fryer.

5. **Air Fry:**
   - Air fry the chicken nuggets at 375°F (190°C) for 10-12 minutes, flipping them halfway through the cooking time. Cook until the nuggets are golden brown and cooked through.

6. **Mist with Cooking Spray:**
   - About halfway through the cooking time, open the air fryer and mist the chicken nuggets with cooking spray. This step helps enhance the crispiness.

7. **Serve Warm:**
   - Once done, transfer the crispy chicken nuggets to a serving plate. Serve the nuggets warm with ketchup, honey mustard, or your preferred sauce, and enjoy!

Chicken Quesadillas

Ingredients:

- 1 lb boneless, skinless chicken breasts, cooked and shredded
- 1 tablespoon olive oil
- 1 small onion, finely diced
- 1 bell pepper, diced
- 2 cloves garlic, minced
- 1 teaspoon ground cumin
- Salt and pepper to taste
- 4 large flour tortillas
- 2 cups shredded cheese (cheddar, Monterey Jack, or a blend)
- Cooking spray or olive oil spray
- Optional toppings: salsa, sour cream, guacamole

Instructions:

1. **Preheat Air Fryer:**

    - Preheat your air fryer to 375°F (190°C).

2. **Sauté Vegetables and Chicken:**

    - In a skillet over medium heat, sauté the diced onions and peppers in olive oil until softened (3-5 minutes). Add minced garlic and cook for an additional minute.

3. **Season and Mix Ingredients:**

    - Add ground cumin, salt, and pepper to the shredded chicken mixture. Mix well and add to the onions and pepper to cook for an additional 3-5 minutes until the chicken is heated through.

4. **Assemble Quesadillas:**

    - Place one tortilla on a clean surface. Spoon a portion of the chicken mixture onto one half of the tortilla, leaving a small border. Sprinkle a generous amount of shredded cheese over the chicken. Fold the tortilla in half to create a half-moon shape, pressing down gently to seal the edges. Repeat with remaining tortillas and chicken mixture.

5. **Air Fry Quesadillas:**

    - Lightly spray the air fryer basket with cooking spray or use an olive oil spray. Place the quesadillas in the air fryer basket, ensuring they are not touching each other.

6. **Flip and Continue Cooking:**

    - Cook in the preheated air fryer for 6-8 minutes, flipping halfway through, or until the quesadillas are golden brown and crispy.

7. **Slice and Serve:**

    - Remove the quesadillas from the air fryer and let them cool for a minute before slicing them into wedges and serve with your favourite topping.

Corn Cob Ribs

Ingredients:

- 4 ears of corn, husked and cleaned
- 2 tablespoons olive oil
- 1 teaspoon smoked paprika
- 1 teaspoon garlic powder
- 1/2 teaspoon onion powder
- 1/2 teaspoon cumin
- Salt and black pepper, to taste
- Optional: Lime wedges for serving

Instructions:

1. **Preheat the Air Fryer:**
   - Preheat your air fryer to 375°F (190°C) for a few minutes.

2. **Cut the Corn:**
   - Cut each ear of corn into halves or thirds, depending on your preference and the size of your air fryer basket. This will create rib-sized pieces.

3. **Prepare the Seasoning Mixture:**
   - In a bowl, combine olive oil, smoked paprika, garlic powder, onion powder, cumin, salt, and black pepper. Mix well to create a seasoning mixture.

4. **Coat the Corn Cob Ribs:**
    - Brush each piece of corn with the seasoning mixture, ensuring they are evenly coated.

5. **Arrange in the Air Fryer Basket:**
    - Place the seasoned corn cob ribs in the air fryer basket in a single layer. You may need to cook in batches depending on the size of your air fryer.

6. **Air Fry:**
    - Air fry the corn cob ribs at 375°F (190°C) for 15-20 minutes, turning them halfway through the cooking time. Cook until the corn is tender and has a nice char.

7. **Serve:**
    - Once done, transfer the corn cob ribs to a serving plate. Squeeze lime wedges over the top if desired.

Roasted Cauliflower

Ingredients:

- 1 medium-sized cauliflower, cut into florets
- 2 tablespoons olive oil
- 1 teaspoon garlic powder
- 1 teaspoon onion powder
- 1/2 teaspoon smoked paprika
- 1/2 teaspoon ground cumin
- 1/2 teaspoon salt, or to taste
- 1/4 teaspoon black pepper
- Optional: Fresh parsley, chopped, for garnish

Instructions:

1. **Preheat the Air Fryer:**
    - Preheat your air fryer to 400°F (200°C) for a few minutes.

2. **Prepare the Cauliflower:**
    - Cut the cauliflower into bite-sized florets. Discard the tough stem.

3. **Season the Cauliflower:**
    - In a large bowl, toss the cauliflower florets with olive oil, garlic powder, onion powder, smoked paprika, ground cumin, salt, and black pepper. Ensure the cauliflower is evenly coated with the seasonings.

4. **Arrange in the Air Fryer Basket:**

    - Place the seasoned cauliflower in the air fryer basket in a single layer. You may need to cook in batches depending on the size of your air fryer.

5. **Air Fry:**

    - Air fry the cauliflower at 400°F (200°C) for 15-20 minutes, shaking the basket or tossing the cauliflower halfway through the cooking time. Cook until the cauliflower is golden brown and crispy at the edges.

Caramelized Bananas

Ingredients:

- 4 ripe bananas, peeled and sliced
- 2 tablespoons unsalted butter, melted
- 2 tablespoons brown sugar
- 1 teaspoon vanilla extract
- 1/2 teaspoon ground cinnamon
- A pinch of salt
- Vanilla ice cream or whipped cream for serving (optional)

Instructions:

1. **Preheat the Air Fryer:**

    - Preheat your air fryer to 350°F (180°C) for a few minutes.

2. **Prepare the Bananas:**

    - Slice the ripe bananas into 1/2-inch thick rounds.

3. **Create the Caramel Sauce:**

    - In a bowl, mix together the melted butter, brown sugar, vanilla extract, ground cinnamon, and a pinch of salt. Stir until the sugar is dissolved.

4. **Coat the Bananas:**
    - Gently toss the banana slices in the caramel sauce, ensuring they are evenly coated.

5. **Arrange in the Air Fryer Basket:**
    - Place the caramel-coated banana slices in the air fryer basket in a single layer. You may need to cook them in batches.

6. **Air Fry:**
    - Air fry the bananas at 350°F (180°C) for 5-7 minutes, shaking the basket halfway through the cooking time. Cook until the bananas are tender and caramelized.

7. **Serve Warm:**
    - Once done, transfer the caramelized banana slices to a serving dish. For an extra indulgence, serve the caramelized bananas warm with a scoop of vanilla ice cream or a dollop of whipped cream

Speedy S'mores

Ingredients:

- 8 graham crackers
- 4 large marshmallows
- 4 squares of chocolate (milk chocolate or your favorite chocolate)
- Cooking spray or mist

Instructions:

1. **Preheat the Air Fryer:**
    - Preheat your air fryer to 375°F (190°C) for a few minutes.

2. **Assemble the S'mores:**
    - Place half of the graham crackers in the air fryer basket. On each cracker, stack a piece of chocolate and a marshmallow.

3. **Top with More Graham Crackers:**
    - Place the remaining graham crackers on top of the marshmallows to complete the s'mores.

4. **Air Fry:**
    - Lightly mist the top of the s'mores with cooking spray. Air fry the assembled s'mores at 375°F (190°C) for 3-5 minutes or until the marshmallows are golden brown and gooey. Keep an eye on them to prevent burning.

5. **Serve Warm:**
    - Once done, carefully remove the s'mores from the basket and allow them to cool for a couple of minutes before eating.

Cinnamon Apple Chips

Ingredients:

- 2-3 large apples (use sweet varieties like Honeycrisp or Gala)
- 1 tablespoon lemon juice
- 1 teaspoon ground cinnamon
- Optional: 1-2 teaspoons sugar (for a sweeter option)
- Cooking spray or mist

Instructions:

1. **Preheat the Air Fryer:**
   - Preheat your air fryer to 375°F (190°C) for a few minutes.

2. **Prepare the Apples:**
   - Core and thinly slice the apples using a mandolin or a sharp knife. Aim for slices that are about 1/8-inch thick. If desired, leave the peel on for added texture and nutrition.

3. **Toss with Lemon Juice:**
   - In a bowl, toss the apple slices with lemon juice. This helps prevent browning and adds a hint of citrus flavor.

4. **Season the Apple Slices:**
    - In a separate bowl, mix ground cinnamon with sugar if using. Coat the apple slices in the cinnamon-sugar mixture, ensuring they are evenly coated.

5. **Arrange in the Air Fryer Basket:**
    - Place the seasoned apple slices in the air fryer basket in a single layer. You may need to cook in batches depending on the size of your air fryer.

6. **Air Fry:**
    - Air fry the apple slices at 375°F (190°C) for 8-10 minutes, flipping or shaking the basket halfway through the cooking time. Cook until the apple chips are golden brown and have a crispy texture.

7. **Cool and Serve:**
    - Once done, transfer the air-fried apple chips to a cooling rack. They will continue to crisp up as they cool.

My Notes

Printed in Great Britain
by Amazon